NEAL CARLIN

FAVOURITE
CELTIC SAINTS
A SIMPLE BOOK OF PRAYERS

VERITAS

This edition published 2010 by
Veritas Publications
7–8 Lower Abbey Street
Dublin 1, Ireland
Email publications@veritas.ie
Website www.veritas.ie

ISBN 978 1 84730 219 9
Copyright © Neal Carlin, 2010

10 9 8 7 6 5 4 3 2 1

A catalogue record for this book is available from the British
Library.

Image of Ireland © Neil Carrigan.
Images throughout © Maurice Harron.

Printed in the Republic of Ireland by Walsh Colour Print,
Kerry

Veritas books are printed on paper made from the wood pulp
of managed forests. For every tree felled, at least one tree is
planted, thereby renewing natural resources.

Contents

ba Dia
an
bniacan.
Coin 1:2

© Neil Carrigan

INTRODUCTION

Two pieces of Church history have always inspired me. One is the Acts of the Apostles, in which is detailed the faith, courage and community lifestyle that existed among the early Christians. 'Every day they continued to meet together in the temple courts. They broke bread in their homes and ate together with glad and sincere hearts, praising God and enjoying the favour of all the people. And the Lord added to their number daily those who were being saved' (Acts 2:46-47). What an image of shared new life in Christ our Saviour!

The other is 'the Golden Age of Ireland' (fifth – twelfth century) when hundreds of 'saints' built small church communities, giving place names to Ireland's townlands and villages. They also evangelised and revitalised Britain and the rest of Europe. They brought the light of the living Lord and dispelled the Dark Ages that followed the collapse of the Roman Empire.

We present these brief 'facts' of the saints' lives and prayers with a two-fold purpose: to honour the men and women of Ireland's Golden Age and thus glorify God; and to renew interest in the characteristics of Celtic Spirituality, so that we, using them as our model, will be renewed.

Today the churches in Ireland need to present the treasures of the faith in Christ Jesus in a way that will give life to our people, young and old. We need new wine skins to present the new wine of the Spirit of Love, Truth and Joy. We need renewed structures to simply present the fullness of Christ and his message. The Lord is building new, authentic Christian communities.

Our own Columba Community, founded in 1981 and built on the charisms of Columba (Colmcille), is an example of a modern Christian community of prayer and reconciliation. In such communities the spirit and teachings of Vatican II documents are being implemented in a very real way. This model of Church, which allows for lay participation and is open to respond to the needs of our age in apostolic ways, certainly requires the attention of anyone seeking to live a full Christian life. If we are to have the credibility, accountability and confidence of the searching people, it would seem that alternative systems of governance, like the ones that Columba and his contemporaries had, are required. This booklet calls us to listen to the Word of God and to obey it radically as did our predecessor, Patrick. God chose to call Patrick to 'come back and walk once more among us'. He started a fire of the Holy Spirit at Slane that burned brightly through the land. His fire was carried by men and women throughout the Continent, the known world at that time.

The Columba Community has been blessed by God. We now have four apostolic centres, including the Celtic Peace Garden. This community is modelled on the Acts of the Apostles and on the ancient Celtic monastic system. Yet because God is always doing a new thing, he spoke a fresh word to inspire this new foundation. This booklet on the Celtic Saints was first written as a guidebook for the pilgrim visiting the recently constructed Celtic Peace Garden on the Donegal/Derry border. Here the pilgrim is invited to walk the six-acre site 'around Ireland' and rediscover our common Christian heritage. Here we offer the characteristics of those men and women of the Golden Age, an age that pre-dates Reformation and counter-Reformation structures and thinking. The love of nature, hospitality, com-

munity-centred (*Muintearas*), Scripture-centred spirituality and art of the Celtic mindset is attracting many visitors from all denominations to our Celtic Garden. Our DVD on the beautiful Celtic Garden and Walk with the Saints of Ireland is available for purchase (see contact details below).

May the Lord, through the lives and ideals promoted by our predecessors, inspire our people again, especially our searching youth so that they experience the light of Christ and become light-bearers in renewed Christian communities throughout this land. May he inspire you, the reader, to listen to his voice and lead you to rebuild his church as he did through Columba, and indeed St Francis.

Enjoy this booklet by reading it slowly and reflectively. May it inspire you to pray with scripture and to fall in love again with the One who loves you and all of us.

Neal Carlin
January 2010

IOSAS Centre, Derryvane, Muff, Co. Donegal
074 9384866   goldenagecentre@hotmail.com
www.columbacommunity.com

St Ita

15 JANUARY

Born near Waterford City, c. AD475, St Ita was baptised Deirdre.

It is said that St Brendan was a pupil of St Ita's and that she told him of three things that were important and pleasing to God: True Faith, Simplicity of Life and Generosity of Spirit.

Ita lived a life of austerity, and by fasting developed a great prayer life. The child Jesus appeared to her and she sang a lullaby to him. Ita formed a praying community at Kileedy, Co. Limerick, where many young people came to join her. She is known as the foster mother of the saints of Ireland.

PRAYER

*Lord, we thank you for giving Ita the passionate love for
    you that allowed her to give up everything for you.*

*May your love put a zeal and a fire
    in our hearts as young people,
    so that we too may sing a new song to you;
    that we may be enthusiastic about life,
    filled with God,
    and not waste time with greed.*

May we listen to you for our calling.

St Brigid

St Brigid was born in Co. Louth c. AD457.

Brigid, as with the Celtic saints generally, was a lover of nature, a carer of the earth and the animal kingdom. Indeed in recent times, those worried about pollution of the earth invoke Brigid's intercession for aid. Brigid was also a patron of the poor. She saw Jesus in the face of every person she met. Her gift of love for the poor is recorded in stories of her giving away what the wealthier members of the community gave to her. One of the many miracles recorded by Cogitosus, writing about one hundred years after Brigid's death, speaks of how God replenished all the butter Brigid had taken from her mother's house to give to the poor! Surely she calls us back to that hospitality for which our golden age was renowned.

One of the memorable practices that continues throughout Ireland is the making of the Brigid Cross. St Brigid intertwined rushes at the deathbed of a chieftain while telling him about Jesus' death on the cross and the work of salvation. The chieftain believed and was baptised into Christ before his death.

PRAYER

Lord, be merciful to me, a sinner.
Give me the humility to kneel before you and confess my sins.
Give me the joy of being unburdened, set free and forgiven.

'Confess your sins to one another and pray for one another for
the healing of your souls.' (James 5:16)

Lord, on the cross you won grace greater than my sin.
Your forgiveness of me glorifies the Father
more than my good deeds can.
I accept your mercy.
You invite me out of exile into community.
I accept your offer of life.
I accept your offer of freedom in a loving, believing
Christian community.

You wash me clean; where sin has abounded
now grace more abounds, for your mercy is
greater than my sin.
I rejoice with Mary's Magnificat:

'My soul proclaims the greatness of the Lord and my spirit
exults in God my Saviour.' (cf. Luke 1:45-56)

St Mura

11 MARCH

St Mura was born in Co. Donegal c. AD550.

St Mura was appointed Abbot of Fahan by Columba. He was a member of the O'Neill clan, which once held the High Kingship of Ireland. Mura wrote many works including chronicles and a rhymed life of Columba. His bell and crozier still survive today and St Mura's cross can be seen at the site of his former monastery in the village of Fahan, Co. Donegal.

Mura's successor, St Fothad na Canoine, was responsible for ensuring that Celtic woman and clerics were no longer conscripted to fight in battles.

PRAYER

Lord, we believe in the Trinity
  and in the Unity of God's people.
Teach your Church – Catholic, Protestant and Orthodox –
  to repent of violence in our histories.

As we look at your early followers who practiced non-violence,
  who died rather than kill,
  guide us to trust you.

May we as Christians promote the way of forgiveness and
  peace.

'They shall beat their swords into ploughshares and their
  spears into pruning hooks; nation shall not lift sword
  against nation, neither shall they learn war anymore.'
  (ISAIAH 2:4)

St Aengus & St Maelruain

11 MARCH AND 7 JULY
CÉILE DÉ – SERVANTS OF GOD

The Céile Dé Reform Movement was founded by Aengus of Clonenagh and Maelruain of Tallaght in the eighth century.

St Aengus and St Maelruain inspired their followers with a love of renunciation and radical monasticism. Religious poetry and liturgy, like the Stowe Missal, flourished at that time.

PRAYER

Lord, as every human system contains the seeds of decay, teach us always to seek renewal, repentance and reform.

Show us what it means in our gatherings to prepare 'new wineskins for the new wine' of your Spirit.

Teach us, Lord, like you, to do only what we see the Father doing.

May our food also be to do the will of the Father.

'These kind are cast out by prayer and fasting.' (MATTHEW 17:21)

St Patrick

17 MARCH

St Patrick, the patron saint of Ireland, is said to have been born in AD385 in Bannavem Taberniae, Western Britain. Conflicting dates are given for his death, c. AD460/490.

Patrick was captured as a boy by Irish raiders and taken to Ireland where he was sold as a slave. Slemish (where Patrick is said to have worked as a shepherd while a slave), Croagh Patrick and Slane all call us to come aside to listen, to fast and pray and get ready to climb the holy mountain and come closer to God in prayer.

As a slave at Slemish, Patrick heard the voice of the Spirit praying inside him. He says, 'I did not know who it was at first' but the Spirit of the Lord spoke and Patrick realised the truth of the scripture that speaks of the prayer being a work of God in us.

Again in a dream Patrick heard the voice of the Irish say, 'Young man, come and walk once more among us'. Again he obeyed and came to preach to a pagan people the Good News of Salvation through Jesus Christ. He was betrayed by a clerical friend and ordered by his Church leadership to come home. Patrick in prayer, however, heard the Lord tell him to 'pay no attention' to those leaders, and, with a charismatic leadership, to continue on in his good work among the Irish.

The word of God is quoted over one hundred times in Patrick's own work, his *Confessions*. God's Holy Spirit speaking to him led Patrick into freedom. As an obedient listener, Patrick can be a great inspiration for the Church in Ireland today. We need to hear the Lord and find a way to new freedom.

PRAYER

Lord, you are the exile ender. You invite me to break free from my sin through repentance and confession.

Thank you for your mercy, which brings me back into the unity and community from which sin exiled me.

'Christ shield me this day
Christ on my right,
Christ on my left,
Christ when I lie down,
Christ when I arise,
Christ in every eye that sees me
and in every ear that hears me.
Christ in the heart of everyone who thinks of me,
Christ on the lips of everyone who speaks of me.'

(FROM *St Patrick's Breastplate*)

St Enda

21 MARCH

Born in Co. Meath, St Enda founded the early Irish monasteries on the Aran Islands.

Though a fierce warrior in his youth, St Enda was persuaded by his sister Franchea (founder of a community of nuns) to change his violent ways and be ordained. He studied in Scotland in Candida Casa Monastery, founded by Ninian at Whithorn in Galloway. Like the famous Clonmacnoise founded by Ciarán, Aran, with its great tradition of austerity, holiness and learning, provided monks, learned men and missionaries for the European continent for five hundred years.

Enda died in his little rock cell by the sea around AD530. The *Martyrdom of Oengus* says, 'It will never be known until the day of judgement the number of saints whose bodies lie in the soil of Aran'.

PRAYER

Lord, Enda would say to us in your words, 'This is the hour, this is the day of salvation, now is the acceptable time to find New Life; to start or join new Christian communities with the fullness and richness of your teaching'.

Give us the grace to accept a radical, Christ-centred life like Enda.

Let Christ be our inspiration in forsaking violence.

Let us today decide to pray together, to share in community our dreams and talents; to spread love, the way of salvation and forgiveness; to be open to oppose our materialistic world.

St Brendan

the Voyager

13 MAY

Born near Fenit, Co. Kerry, c. AD484, Brendan is one of the early Irish monastic saints.

Brendan was a pupil of St Ita's, and after his tutelage set out on voyages to the continent with a company of monks, pilgrims, explorers and missionaries, in search, it is said, of a paradise. Legend has it that Brendan landed his ship on what he thought was an island but in fact turned out to be the back of a whale, who allowed Brendan to shore there and conduct Easter Mass.

PRAYER

Lord, I come like Brendan the Voyager, the pilgrim, always searching to discover you afresh in new places in your creation.

Your ancient missionaries travelled over land and sea without rest.

The Irish saints left this land to bring the good news to the whole known world.

Teach me that the One I seek is the One who causes me to seek.

You, Lord, are my source and my soul's desire.

Teach me to rest in you, the cause of my search.

St Dymphna
of Gheel, Belgium

15 MAY

St Dymphna, a seventh century saint, was born in Co. Monaghan.

Dymphna fled to Gheel in Belgium because of her father's unnatural attentions. She devoted herself to looking after the poor and sick, especially the mentally ill, until her father found her. Within days of Dymphna's slaying, the mentally and emotionally disturbed found healing at her graveside.

The local bishop commissioned a *Life of Dymphna* to be written in the thirteenth century. For centuries Gheel was noted for its care and treatment of the mentally ill. 'God does not withdraw his gifts', as scripture tells us.

St Dymphna's Well in Culdavnet, Co. Monaghan, was and still is a major place of pilgrimage.

PRAYER

Lord, thank you for Dymphna's gifts of chastity and love of the sick.

Inspire your young women and men to give their lives in caring for others.

Raise up today new members of Christian communities who will build your kingdom.

Teach us how best to serve your poor and hungry, both mentally and spiritually.

The hearts and minds of all of us need to be cleansed.

We need to be fed with your values, your mind and your holy will if we are to grow to be fully alive and free.

Teach us how to fast, to pray and to discern your will.

St Kevin
of Glendalough

3 JUNE

St Kevin was born at Fort of the White Fountain, Leinster, c. AD498.

Kevin lived as a hermit for seven years in a cave at Glendalough, Co. Wicklow. Now situated there is a Bronze Age tomb known as St Kevin's Bed, to which he was reportedly led by an angel. He wore animal skins, ate the nettles and herbs that came to hand, and spent his time in prayer. Word of his holiness spread and he attracted many followers.

When Kevin saw that the monastery at Glendalough was well established, he withdrew to live again as a hermit. Four years later, however, he returned to Glendalough at the entreaty of his monks, and served as abbot until his death at age 120.

Kevin was renowned for his patience; a story is told that a bird once laid an egg in the palm of his hand. Kevin, not wanting to harm the egg, remained motionless until the egg was hatched.

PRAYER

'Come apart with me into a desert place and rest
   awhile.' (MARK 6:31)

'Be still and know that I am God.' (PSALM 46:10)

Lord, you speak to me in the depth and silence of my heart.
May I reflect daily.
Purify my intentions.

St Columba
(Colmcille)

9 JUNE

St Columba (Colmcille) was born in Gartan, Co. Donegal, in AD521.

There are many prophecies, visions and miracles recorded in St Adamnan's (Eunan) book on the life of Columba. Central to the great apostolate of Columba was his missionary work of converting the Picts to Christianity. In the Donegal/Derry area, Columba is remembered for his great work of reconciliation between the Scottish and Irish parts of the kingdom of Dalriada. His convention at Drumceat, Limavady (AD575) ensured peace between King Aed and King Aidan, his counterpart in Scotland whom Columba had crowned king on Iona. Columba also defended the bards at Drumceat, where many of the chieftains were offended by their lifestyle, poems and songs. Columba negotiated on behalf of these songsters and won the title 'Patron of the Bards' for his great work of reconciliation.

Columba loved to build in close proximity to oak groves because of their natural beauty, hence his choice of Derry and Durrow for his monastic settlements in Ireland. Columba was Ireland's first great missionary. His last written words were: 'Those who seek the Lord shall want for no manner of good thing.' He died on the Scottish island of Iona in AD597.

Columba's last words to his brothers were:
'Have unfeigned love for one another with peace. If you keep this course according to the examples of the holy men and women of old, God, who strengthens the good, will help you, and I, dwelling with him, shall intercede for you.'

PRAYER

Lord, we thank you for our great patron, Columba.

Increase your people's love of your word and your presence in the Holy Eucharist.

Teach us to be reconcilers like Columba.
Teach us to pray in your Spirit.
Teach us how to build Christian communities and to be on fire with your presence.

Give us a great love for the outsider and welcome them home. Let us live in the Trinity of Love.

Saint Ciarán
of Saighir

14 JUNE

Born on Clear Island off Co. Cork, St Ciarán is said to be the first born of the Irish saints.

Often referred to as Ciarán the Elder, St Ciarán founded a monastery on Clear Island. It is said that he healed a small stricken bird after it was wounded by a hawk. The patron of the diocese of Ossory, Ciarán was the founder of Saighir (Seir-Kieran) in what is now Co. Offaly.

PRAYER

Lord, we thank you for creation and for wild beauty.

You chose to pray, often all night long in the garden.

Your saints from our country sought to meet you in places like this.

Please send your spirit to be with us on this journey.

Open our eyes to the wonder of your presence in nature and in the footsteps of your holy men and women.

Let me meet you. Let me know your guidance, your peace, your forgiveness and your love.

As I tread this, your earth, give me reverence for all your creatures, for your people, for all I see or encounter along the way.

St Killian

of Wurzburg, Germany

8 JULY

Killian was born in Mullagh, Co. Cavan, c. AD40.

Killian travelled to eastern Franconia and Thuringia along with eleven companions, and having preached the gospel in Wurzburg, he succeeded in converting the local lord, Duke Gozbert, to Christianity. Killian told the Duke that he was in violation of sacred scripture by being married to his brother's widow. Upon hearing this, the widow ordered that he be beheaded along with his two companions. He was martyred with fellow monks, Colman and Totnan, at Wurzburg, Germany, in AD89.

The New Testament belonging to Killian was preserved in the Cathedral of the Saviour until 1803, when it was removed and placed in the University Library in Wurzburg. Following in the footsteps of Killian, some six hundred Irish monks went to preach and live in Bavaria from the seventh to the ninth century.

PRAYER

*Thank you, Lord, for the courage and missionary spirit of
Killian and his companions.*

*Give us zeal to seek first your kingdom and to go forth with
faith in your guidance, to live the Gospel with courage.*

St Attracta

11 AUGUST

St Attracta lived at the same time as St Patrick and received the veil from him.

St Attracta was a native of Co. Sligo. She resolved to devote herself to God, but being opposed by her parents, fled to South Connaught and made her first foundation near Boyle, Co. Roscommon, where she lived as a hermitess.

She moved to Killaraght in Coolavin, Co. Sligo, and a large village grew up around her oratory there. St Attracta then set up a hospice for travellers, which existed there until 1539.

The cup and cross of St Attracta were venerated in Killaraght, and her feast day of 11 August is celebrated in the diocese of Achonry, of which she is the patroness.

Many miracles were attributed to her. She was renowned for her charity and hospitality and is known as the foundress of several churches in Galway and Sligo.

PRAYER

Lord, we give you thanks for the great gifts of hospitality and works of mercy which Attracta had in abundance.

I open my hands and my heart to receive these gifts.

Help me to show hospitality to strangers.

'Let hospitality be your special care.' (ROMANS 12:13)

St Fiacre
of Meaux, France

Born c. AD600, Fiacre left Ireland and arrived in France c. AD626.

When he arrived in France, Fiacre was befriended by the local bishop Faro and soon became famous for healing.

So often did he cure ulcers, they became better known as St Fiacre's disease. He built a hospice for Irish pilgrims beside his monastery and was noted for his cultivation of medicinal herbs. He died c. AD676.

PRAYER

Lord, thank you for pure and uncontaminated food; for health of body; for healing of ulcers and diseases.

We offer you thanks, God our Creator.

All you created you saw was good.

Forgive our greed and our poisoning of the earth for short-term gains.

Teach us patience and love of its soil.

St Eunan
(Adamnan)

23 SEPTEMBER

Eunan was born in Drumhome, Co. Donegal, c. AD624.

The ninth abbot of Iona, Eunan assisted at the Synod of Tara in AD697. There the Canon of Adamnan was adopted, which allowed children and women freedom from being engaged in war.

He wrote the *Life of Columba*, the most complete piece of biography of Columba, boasted of throughout Europe up to the Middle Ages. He introduced the Roman Paschal Observance despite opposition, especially from his fellow Celtic monks in Iona.

PRAYER

Lord, we thank you for the written word on Columba, which inspired his followers in faith.

Teach us to know you, not just to know about you.

Teach us to reverence your living word.

You spoke through Adamnan to safeguard children and women from war.

Bless and protect the weak and defend us from violence and danger.

As we read about Columba in Eunan's story, let us have 'unfeigned love for one another' as fellow disciples of Christ.

Teach us to be real missionaries among our own people.

St Canice

11 OCTOBER

St Canice was born in Glengiven near Limavady, Co. Derry c. AD515.

St Canice was Columba's friend and a great intercessor.

He was descended from Ui-Dalainn, a Waterford tribe, and his father was a distinguished bard, who made his way northwards and settled at Glengiven. Tradition has it that Canice founded a monastery in Kilkenny, where a round tower and cathedral bear his name. A man of great eloquence and learning, he wrote a commentary on the gospels, known as *Glas-Chainnigh*.

He calls us to *Muintearas* – Community. As no man is an island, we all need to share our gifts for the building of the Kingdom. We belong together as we gaze at the image of the Risen Christ.

PRAYER

Lord, you are really present here.

Give me the grace to respect that.

When I call, answer me, teach me to listen.

Speak, Lord – your servant is listening, for you hear the cry of the poor.

I am empty and here; please fill me with your riches.

Have mercy on me, a sinner. Take me out of loneliness and into Muintearas – Community.

St Gall
of Switzerland

St Gall was born c. AD550.

From Leinster, Gall travelled to Europe with his friend, Columbanus. They parted company acrimoniously at Bregenz, Switzerland in AD621.

Gall built a hermitage beside the River Steinach and it is there he is said to have ordered a bear to collect firewood for him in the woods. Gall's small monastery became a mighty medieval library and university. In St Gallen in Switzerland, named after the saint, there are around one hundred books on display in old Irish and Latin. Gall died at Arbon in AD640. He represents how the Irish saved civilization after the Dark Ages following the fall of Rome.

PRAYER

Lord, we thank you for learning.

You who 'advanced in wisdom and in age',
    teach us to study your word,
    to listen to your voice of wisdom,
    to respect the sacred books of scripture
    and the wonders of modern science.

St Columbanus
of Luxeuil and Bobbio

23 NOVEMBER

St Columbanus was born in Leinster c. AD543.

The most influential of the Celtic missionaries who chose 'exile for Christ' on the European mainland, St Columbanus sailed for Europe, arriving in Brittany.

He and his followers quickly established a reputation for their preaching and piety and founded a monastery in the Vosges Mountains. Columbanus eventually settled in Bobbio, Italy, where there is now a cathedral honouring his memory. He died in a cave while on a prayer vigil, leaving his staff to his friend Gall as a sign of reconciliation.

PRAYER

Lord, you inspired Columbanus, a handsome young man, to forsake all for you.

He spread the Good News in the known world with courage, wisdom and love.

*Raise up in Ireland young men and women like Columbanus to seek first the true homeland of heaven,
to build with your inspiration your kingdom on earth,
to confront error and to always seek reconciliation.*